Drawing BONES

My 15 Years of Cartooning
Brian Mulroney
by
Aislin

Canadian Cataloguing in Publication Data

Aislin
   Drawing bones

ISBN 1-55013-392-6

1. Mulroney, Brian, 1939 -   -Caricatures and cartoons.
2. Canada-   Politics and government - 1984-   -Caricatures and cartoons.*
3. Canadian wit and humor, Pictorial.   I. Title.
NC1449.A58A4 1991   971.064'7'092   C91-094825-9

Key Porter Books Limited
70 The Esplanade
Toronto, Ontario
Canada M5E 1R2

Typesetting: First Image

Printed and bound in Canada

91 92 93 94 95 6 5 4 3 2 1

Contents

Preface

Drawing Bones is a selection of cartoons I've drawn of Brian Mulroney during the past fifteen years.

Without my planning it or having any premonition of what would unfold, Mulroney has become of special interest to me as I have been in approximately the same place he has at similar times for the last twenty-five years.

We both arrived in Montreal in the 1960s after studying at universities in Quebec City. Not together, mind you; and the one off-the-rack suit between us, Brian owned. Nevertheless, our different activities often took place in the same milieu.

This is not an exposé of Brian Mulroney. We aren't friends. But I became a Bones watcher very early on, and it benefitted me in caricaturing him.

At one time I thought René Lévesque was my true cartooning *raison d'être*. But, when push came to shove, I respected René too much to be as cruel as I might. As it turned out, I'd been sharpening my pencil on René to skewer Brian. We are always sharpest when satirizing our own.

Anna Porter and Phyllis Bruce at Key Porter Books asked if I would write some commentary for this book: how I go about cartooning Mulroney; how the process works; and how my thinking about him, and about cartooning him, has evolved over the years. At least, I think that's what they wanted me to write.

The project allowed me to remember people and events,

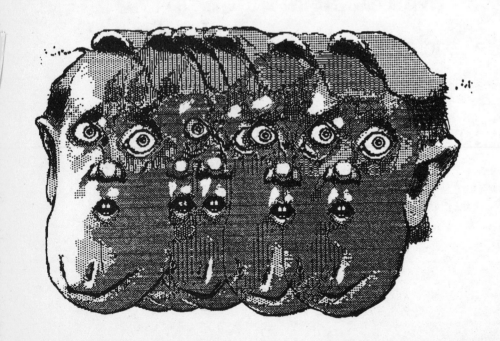

their aftermath and my reaction at the time. Without intending to do so, I seem to have written something of a summing up of my career to date, centred on my favourite target. If the reader finds this somewhat self-indulgent, I apologize; there are plenty of funny pictures to look at.

Writing isn't the medium I'm used to. A keyboard does not breathe for me the way a brush can. When I draw, a situation or a facial expression comes easily; pumping out adjectives and subordinate clauses is a clumsier process.

So, thanks, first, go to Charis Wahl for adding finesse in editing this text and understanding how important it was to get this sounding — well — like me, contradictions and all.

Thanks also to all the people in the libraries at *The Gazette* and *The Toronto Star*.

Being left-handed, I couldn't keep things running smoothly without my right hand in Montreal, Peter Arsenault. Anne Doris at *The Toronto Star* has become invaluable in the few short months I've been there, particularly in helping me to understand "les Torontois" a little better.

I also thank John Honderich and Haroon Siddiqui at *The Toronto Star* for allowing me to pay less attention than I should have to drawing editorial-page cartoons for them while I wrote this.

Finally, this book is dedicated to Joan Fraser, my editor at *The Gazoo*, and to fifteen mutual years of Bones watching.

A First Look at This Guy Called Bones

Thankfully, politicians are usually avoidable.

Unlike journalists, cartoonists need neither scrums nor an executive assistant's ear to earn our daily bread. Our well-connected and educated colleagues dig up the stories, deep-fry them, and dish them up. We cartoonists react, often with heartburn, much as does the general public.

To be completely honest, pols aren't *always* avoidable — I do venture away from my drawing board every few months. At a literary fund-raiser several years ago, Pierre Trudeau and I found ourselves trapped together in the receiving line. There being no escape, we had a brief but civilized chat about Strathmore sketchbooks, the nearest subject to hand. I happened to be carrying one in my hip pocket.

Once, but only once, I sat down with Brian Mulroney, scotch-to-scotch, back when he wasn't active in politics. We were at Les Halles, on Crescent Street, shortly after Brian's first run at the Tory leadership, because Nick Auf der Maur —

journalist, city councillor, failed Marxist, and future Tory candidate — was about to be married.

I was seated between Mulroney and Patrick Brown, now the respected Asia correspondent for CBC and Radio-Canada, but then a fellow rounder, freelance writer, and one of three authors of a small book entitled *Winners,*

Pal Nick

Losers. It had been published by *The Last Post*, a now-defunct leftish publication many of us worked for.

Winners, Losers had been rather sympathetic to Joe Clark and critical of Brian Mulroney. I had illustrated the book with caricatures of all the Tory contenders as wrestlers — this cartoon of Mulroney was the first I had drawn of him.

Forgetting about all this amidst the jolly razzing of the groom-to-be, I introduced Brown and Mulroney.

Brian's face contorted into that petulant-four-year-old expression we now know well.

"You! You wrote that fucking book!" Mulroney roared at Brown. "That book made my mother cry!"

Wondering if Woodward and Bernstein had considered Nixon's mom's feelings, I had a go at damage control.

"Look, Brian, that's our job," I said in Brown's defence. "I drew critical cartoons of *all* you guys."

"Sure, sure," Brian said, "but those were only cartoons."

"Hmmm," I thought. "Only cartoons?"

Avoiding the Dole

I do love Brian Mulroney, but for all the wrong reasons.

There are about thirty-five political cartoonists sprinkled across the country. Our cartoons accompany the newspaper editorials you pretend to read every day. We thrive on miserable news.

Bones is often that, continuing a well-established tradition. Tories and other politicians with conservative leanings have always proved more caricaturable than others: J.W. Bengough caricatured John A. Macdonald throughout most of his political career. John Diefenbaker will always be remembered the way Duncan Macpherson drew him.

Maurice Duplessis, Quebec's strong-man of the 1940s and '50s, was rarely criticized by the press, not in so many words. But cartoonist Robert LaPalme created caricatures so devastating that Duplessis's Union Nationale party offered him a generous scholarship to study art anywhere in the world except Quebec. LaPalme refused.

Not all cartoonists have

LaPalme's grit. When the artform was young, KING GEORGE III paid a caricaturist to stop drawing him as a syphilitic. The royal plan backfired. Other cartoonists started a vicious attack on the King, in the hopes of being paid off, too.

It has been said that humour couldn't exist in a perfect world, though we run no risk of finding out. This is why jokes about Dan Quayle and Brian Mulroney outnumber those about Mother Teresa and June Callwood.

An ideal leader would never lie to us. He or she would inspire us to be bilingual. All races, creeds, and colours — new Canadians and old — would together forge a land to be envied by all. Business would lie down with labour, and unemployment would be a thing of the past.

Well, almost. We thirty-five caricaturists would be out of work.

Trudeau during the October Crisis

8

A Piece of Cake

I cut my cartooning teeth on Pierre Trudeau and René Lévesque. Canadian politics were suddenly interesting, sophisticated, and, at times, refreshingly unpredictable. Not that Canadians had much say in the matter, as two men wrestled over their opposing views of Quebec and Canada.

What a caricaturable duo they were. Pierre's disdain and arrogance were a constant challenge: foxy, intelligent, and — an oddity in Canadian politics — seldom an easy read. Fiery and emotional, Lévesque was a joy to draw. After the PQ election victory in 1976, newspapers around the world suddenly wanted cartoons to illustrate Quebec stories. Lévesque may have scared some Anglos to points west, but he tripled my income.

My style at the time — big heads and little bodies — suited both Trudeau and Lévesque. Both men were balding. Trudeau is a short man; Lévesque was even shorter. (On meeting René, my wife, Carol, was surprised to find the man almost as small as I drew him.)

Both men's physiognomies lent themselves to caricature. If you were to describe the individual features — eyes,

O.K. EVERYBODY TAKE A VALIUM!

P.Q. victory in Quebec

mouths, chins, and so on — the concoction might have seemed ugly, even gargoyle-like. But these were wonderful faces, because of the way they communicated the men's convictions.

Then along came Brian Mulroney, whom *The Edmonton Journal* once described as having Paul Newman eyes, Robert Redford hair, and a chin by Gibraltar. Tall, friendly — a real bib and tucker — always flashing a smile. By definition Mulroney should have been a disaster for cartoonists.

In fact, cartooning him is a piece of cake — he is almost too easy to ridicule. Why? Because Trudeau and Lévesque demanded our respect. Mulroney begs for it.

I first heard of Bones — Mulroney's nickname in the early days — before Trudeau was prime minister. I was working summers on Quebec's artists' alley, Rue du Trésors, drawing portraits and caricatures of tourists for a few dollars each. This kept me fed during winters at l'Ecole des Beaux-Arts.

I was getting to know the small Irish community in Quebec City — I had married one of their own, Carol Devlin — and they all knew about Mulroney, him being Irish *and* and a Progressive Conservative, possibly the first in Canada. (At the time, Brian Mulroney, Lucien Bouchard, and others you'd later find in the financial pages were studying at Université Laval.)

Two of Carol's cousins, Jim and Bill Noonan, ran the Chien d'Or tavern, around the corner from my stoop on the Rue du Trésors. Journalists drank there, and would talk of this boy wonder from time to time, as a diversion from current and upcoming events: Bourassa, Lévesque, the October Crisis, militant unions, separatism, Jean Drapeau and his Olympics, the election of the Parti Québécois, and the referendum.

I caught on with *The Montreal Star*, as the paper was then shopping for a few oddballs who could meet a deadline. This was 1967, after all. In 1972, I moved over to the poorer but livelier *Gazette*, where any number of talented characters were learning their trades. At the time, it seemed, editors drank — and therefore hired other drinkers. Among the cavorting journalists, that name came up again. What was it, anyway?

**"I've always been a frustrated saloon singer."
—Brian Mulroney to Suzanne Somers in Hollywood.**

10

Mul-*ROW*-ney or
Mul-*ROO*-ney?

In the 1970s, intelligent conversation demanded at least a cursory knowledge of Mao or Ché. But Tories? The subject never came up. Having grown up in downtown Montreal and Toronto, I didn't know any Conservatives. My parents were avid fans of the cartoon-strip *Pogo*, which explains them politically, and their friends were similarly liberal-left newspaper people and creative types. She'd never confess it, but my mother, I suspect, may have voted for Diefenbaker — once. After all, she was born in Saskatchewan.

But here was Brian, rapidly making news, first by settling the *La Presse* strike and later, as a member of the high-profile Cliche Commission. And he was getting favourable press, even from some people I knew.

The real news came when Mulroney declared himself a candidate for the Progressive Conservative leadership in 1976. Montreal was curious and I decided to go to my first Tory convention, a kind of political freak show.

The convention should have been an eye-opener, but instead it was my first drunk-

THE MEDIA INTERVIEW THE MEDIA.

SOMEBODY PAY THE BABYSITTER...

up with our national media, who, I discovered, followed the convention, like everyone else, on TV. Larry Zolf had been assigned several Mulroneyettes to babysit; but Larry preferred to talk, and to cheer for fellow maniac Jack Horner. I made it a trio.

I was also delighted when Claude Wagner lost. Wagner was always some piece of work. Somewhere in my files is a letter from his lawyers, sent just after he died in 1979. Under the circumstances, they wrote, they were dropping the libel suit he had started over one of my cartoons.

Bones came third, but established his name by spending a great deal of money. One observer noted that he spent money like a man who didn't have any. He didn't, but coming third gave him time to make some while running Iron Ore, in Montreal, and avoiding the silliness of actually having to run for election.

The winner, Joe Clark, appeared sincere enough but often pitiable up against the crafty Trudeau. In the 1980 election the Tories won one seat in Quebec. *One.* Evidently, a new Quebec strategy was called for.

Suddenly, all of Brian's then best friends — Michael Meighen, Michel Cogger, John Lynch-Staunton, Brian Gallery,

and ring-leader Frank Moores — were smiling. So was Bones, even while embracing Clark prior to the 1982 Tory leadership review at the Ritz-Carlton. His then best friends were busy elsewhere in the hotel.

Joe squeaked through in the review but was honourable — and stupid — enough to call for a leadership convention

anyway. There was a bash thrown at the Queen Elizabeth Hotel in Montreal. Apparently a spontaneous outburst of support for Bones, it was planned right down to the three forks at dinner. "The Friends of Brian Mulroney" night, it was.

And, yes, I went. It amazed me how many people I knew at the party. Many weren't genuine Tories, even though

⇨ THE TORIES-PART TWO...

...FACE FACTS, DAD, WE TORIES HAVE CHANGED!

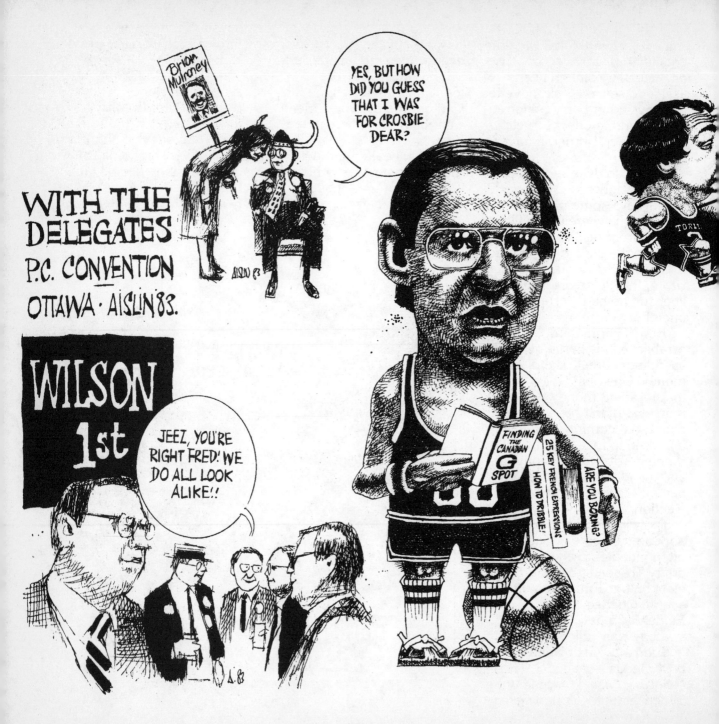

SO WHY DO SOME OF US TRAVEL THOUSANDS OF MILES TO WATCH THIS WHOLE CONVENTION ON TELEVISION IN THE PRESS CLUB AND THEN ALL WRITE THE SAME STORY???

TO GET DRUNK, THAT'S WHY...

they'd all developed that smile. Montrealers could smell a winner.

One person who was both a friend and smiling was Bones's brother Gary, a personable, likeable guy with no previous political experience. We began to avoid certain topics, Gary and I, especially after he went to work for his brother. Sooner or later, we both knew, first things would come first: his loyalty to Brian and my loyalty to my job. Inevitably, they did.

First things for Bones were closing down the town of Schefferville and going to the Tory leadership convention. I would remember more of this one, held on a fine weekend in June.

It seemed inevitable that the Tories' time was rapidly approaching, what with the new conservatism everywhere

and Ronald Reagan so popular in the United States. Whoever won this convention would probably form his team from the other contenders, so I had to watch closely. These guys were my future bread and butter.

In 1976, I had caricatured all of the Tory leadership hopefuls as wrestlers. In 1984, I drew the new slate as basketball players. Don't ask why. Perhaps David Crombie's shortness inspired it. Or the ludicrousness of Canadians trying to play an American game. Bob-sledders or squid-jiggers would have served just as well — anything that suggested that everyone is a team player but with a different quirk and style.

Before the convention, Bones had been asked about what the cartoonists were doing with him.

"I love it," he had responded, "I love what those guys do to my chin!"

Inspired, I paraded his chin in a bra.

I must admit, I really wanted Mulroney to win. The scuttlebutt was that, if he lost, he'd become the next publisher of *The Gazette*.

"Brian! Brian! Brian!"

How I Draw Brian

Cartooning is a genuinely populist artform. Millions of Canadians may see a given cartoon in their newspapers and therefore tend to be curious about how it's done.

"Where do you get your crazy ideas?" they ask.

"I have a great idea for a cartoon. Want to hear it?" Hmmm.

"Are you censored?" No, but ...

"How do politicians react?" Well ... "Do you ever get sued?"

Why don't we just walk through the creation of one cartoon, from beginning to end.

First, What's the Buzz ...

One of the oddities of this job is that being too well informed is not necessarily a good thing. It's better to be frustrated and confused by politics, as many readers are, and to express those feelings for them. If a cartoonist becomes particularly taken up with some aspect of politics, he's likely to do that topic to death, boring people and becoming a propagandist. No matter how good the cause, losing perspective is cartooning death.

We do have to have a general idea of what's going on, but leave the political minutiae to the journalists.

What's most important is the Buzz — how non-insiders feel about everyday events. Duncan Macpherson, the godfather of English-Canadian cartooning, described the cartoon box on the editorial page as "a soapbox to yell back at the machine."

My main source of unadulterated Buzz is any coffee shop first thing in the morning. Moe's, the all-night snack bar known to all Montreal downtowners, and the Mars, on College Street in Toronto, are two particular favourites.

How are people reacting to something? Do they seem amused? Delighted? Appalled? Angered? I eavesdrop while I read the morning papers, assuming that a thousand similar chats are going on in coffee shops everywhere. If I hear several conversations on the same topic, I may very well be on to my topic *du jour*.

I scan seven or eight papers a day, honing in on the news sections and a dozen or so favourite columnists. However, I never read the editorials in *The Gazette* or *The Toronto Star*, the two papers I work for. Don't get me wrong — both papers have exceptional editorialists; but I value my independent opinions and ideas. (This is flagrantly obvious when the slant of a cartoon is diametrically opposed to that expressed in the editorial beside it.)

Television news is a must, but not for hard information. What interests me on TV is not what the politicians are saying — I can read that in tomorrow's newspaper — but how they look saying it.

Incidentally, I truly do enjoy watching Brian Mulroney on the news with Carol. If you want to know when an Irishman is bullshitting, check it out with an Irish woman.

Mind you, the Buzz isn't always foolproof: there have been days when I've picked what seemed to be a good subject, drawn something supposedly hilarious, and then gone home. The next morning people have called, demanding to know what the cartoon meant. So I'd look at it again and, if I didn't quite understand

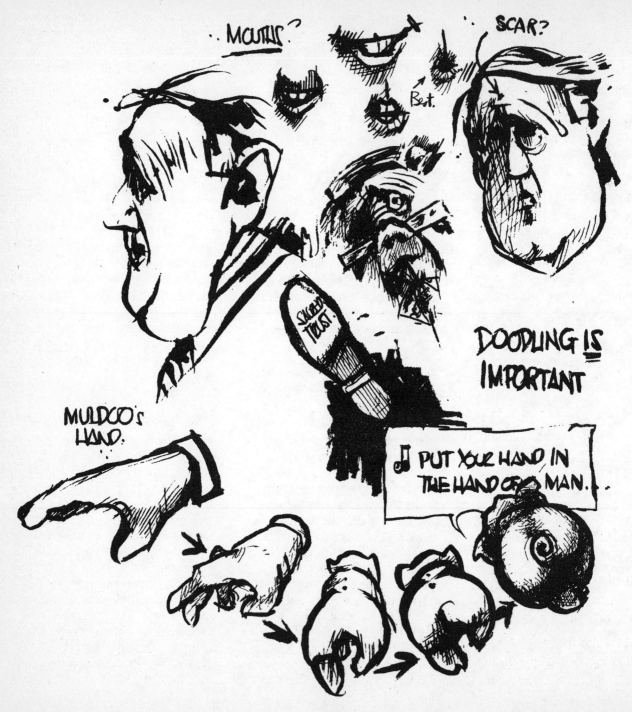

it either, call Carol and ask her what she thought I might have meant by it.

Hey, it happens, but not that often.

Starting a Cartoon

It's Monday, June 17, 1991. Two TV channels led off the news last night with the wrap-up of Mulroney's five-day visit to Germany. All this morning's papers have it on their front pages. As well, there's a statement by Kohl encouraging Canada not to weaken itself "by allowing Quebec to separate."

At the coffee shop, a Francophone snidely wonders what world leader Brian will con into speaking up for Canada next. Kohl's statement, like similar ones made by Bush and others in Mulroney's presence, is being perceived as international interference and domestic opportunism.

Obviously, this is the topic *du jour*.

I don't understand the chemistry that produces cartoon ideas; but, if I follow certain daily routines, they keep coming. (For example, I always take the phone off the hook when I'm working. I never stop, or take a break, until it's finished.) Why ask questions when you're on a roll?

Apart from downing donuts and caffeine and calling it work, I doodle and take preliminary notes. Here are some of the doodles from June 17. Some don't seem very closely related to the final cartoon, but all were very much a part of getting to it.

The Rough

Often I wake up with a cartoon idea taking shape in my mind; but today I don't know yet what the finished cartoon will be. It will develop as I draw and think. (In the crunch, I can always use Duncan Macpherson's offhanded advice: "Terry, if it isn't there, fake it with technique." It's not a bad fall-back position: wow them with the drawing, even if the humour falls flat.)

As a child I drew airplanes for hours on end. I can draw a decent 747 in less than a minute, cross-hatching and all. In my bad old days, pals could always tell when I'd drawn a cartoon hung over: it would be of a plane with a voice balloon coming out of it, saying something silly.

Today I begin by sketching Bones. It's a comfortable thing to do — like stepping into a pair of beat-up shoes. (Several years ago, ten cartoonists were signing books at a store in Toronto. Six of us were left handed. Go figure. It's easy to spot the work of left-handed cartoonists. We tend to place the shading on the left-hand side of the figure or object, so we can see what

...NOW MR. TRUDEAU IS WAVING TO THE CROWD...

we're drawing.)

I think about an angle:

Amazingly, all the time he was in Germany, no scandal erupted, over there or back at home. Draw a sweatingly grateful Muldoon? Kohl at the table as a Canadian constitutional expert? Brian getting other world leaders to speak out "spontaneously" in favour of a united Canada? Good one.

But who? Brian coaxing? Brian begging? Easy enough. Exaggerate to grovelling? Where do I put him? Not in Germany — he's already on his way home. His office. Alone, scheming.

Meanwhile I'm doodling, getting the expression I want.

How to suggest Mulroney scheming? Mouth closed, eyes peering slightly upwards. Shoulders slightly slouched towards his joined hands. Guarded, concentrating. Draw him twiddling his thumbs, some nervous movement to imply planning?

Starting a Second Drawing

Who would Brian be thinking of? Which world leader to speak up on Canada? Move the shoulders up more…. Hide the shirt collar a bit…. Angle the head to the side.

Little additions here and there — a bite out of his ear. (I've been using this lately to suggest him being put upon.) Switch to ink, dry brush. Give head more form.

Have him phoning someone? Or waiting for a call?

Thumbnail of a phone.

Brian's anticipating an important phone call?

Fingers on the receiver, waiting for it to ring. Good — twiddling thumbs are history.

Okay, the final idea's come to me.

Ready to Start the Final Drawing

First I check that no bigger story is breaking. It's safe: my assistant, Peter Arsenault, tells me that, in *The Gazette* cafeteria, all anyone is talking about is Otis Nixon stealing six bases against the Expos last night.

Readers look at a cartoon for an average of seven seconds. If you do it right, they won't notice the things you've incorporated into the drawing to make it easy for them to understand a fairly complicated scenario. When they can read the mood quickly, I've done my job properly.

The big decisions have been made: now we're down to details, such as the telephone.

Is Brian urging all the leaders of western nations to speak up in favor of a united Canada?...

Com'on, Bourassa, you bugger. CALL!

The finished cartoon ... or almost

Suggest waiting for it to ring? Put fingers on the receiver. Grasping. Place two thumbs together.

Does the telephone need to be more obvious? Hang over the border a fraction of an inch.

Add reading glasses, with papers strewn about. Suggest he's ignoring important matters in favour of waiting for this call.

The face now. Emphasize he's nervously waiting this call. Add sweat beads. Good — looks like he's praying and constipated at the same time. A bandage on the other ear? Why not?

Positioning the text was important in this cartoon. The eye automatically starts to read in the top left-hand corner, so I set clear, readable type there to encourage the viewer to read it first. I wanted the punchline in the bubble to be read second, so I hand-lettered the text, smaller and in lower case, making it harder to read than the typeset information.

There, done.

All that's left is to fill in the contours and textures of the drawing. I love to draw, and tend to overdo detail. Then we're left with just a dark blotch when the cartoon is reproduced on newsprint.

The people at the Toronto Star Syndicate, who send my cartoons out to other papers, are always yelling at me: "Draw less! Draw less!"

So, I'm still learning.

The Editor

Finally, my assistant takes the cartoon to the editor for approval and a spell check. (Cartoonists are the world's worst spellers.)

I rarely hear from my editors and can go for weeks without seeing them. But today Joan Fraser of *The Gazette* calls with a small request on this cartoon: Could I remove the word "bugger"?

Now Joan and I have gone to the wall on smaller matters in the past. But I'm feeling generous — "Sure, why not?" — knowing the cartoon was going to appear in this book anyway.

The cartoon as it appeared in the newspaper

The Honeymoon

Mulroney, as the new leader of a political party, had to go through the pedestrian business of actually winning a seat in the House of Commons. A by-election was arranged in a safe Nova Scotia riding, although most any riding in the country would probably have done the job.

High-profile Liberals were flown in to work the crowd, but the party was visibly exhausted. (Of course, as an insider I knew they were through — I had read it in columns by Allan Fotheringham and Peter C. Newman.)

Camelot North appeared to be at hand. And some media people, who'd gone Mulroney bonkers, were in line for the canapés. Bill Fox had always been a competent digger-type reporter; but somehow the hard-nosed scribe had been charmed by Bones. As always, the price for Brian's friendship was total loyalty. So Foxie became Mulroney's head media flak, trading old journalist friends for new, smiling ones.

As *The Toronto Star's* Washington correspondent before jumping to Bones's staff, Fox was the first North American journalist to suggest that Reagan was senile. I

Mulroney with Bill Fox

26

wonder how Bill Fox set up photo-ops for Brian at the White House?

L. Ian MacDonald was a political columnist at *The Gazette,* but he had obviously been riding Brian's train for quite some time. Ian wrote the official biography, *Mulroney: The Making of the Prime Minister.* After that, other *Gaz* journalists became suspicious of Ian. He'd always seemed destined for something other than journalism, and proved it by quitting *The Gazette* to write speeches in the PMO or something.

It seems to me that good journalists always have an "us vs. them" attitude; but there have always been people who leave the media to work for the government. It's a free country — but, after making the jump, perhaps they should never be allowed back. Bill Fox and L. Ian MacDonald have left the PMO. They are now Ottawa "consultants," not far from the teat.

On the other hand, my old pal Nick Auf der Maur also co-wrote a biography of Brian, *The Boy from Baie-Comeau,* which I refuse to read. But I forgive Nick anything, even running for the Tories in 1984. Lucky for us he lost and continues to prop up downtown Montreal, where he belongs.

Mulroney.
L. IAN MacDONALD.
Foreword by M. Richler.

THE BOY FROM BAIE-COMEAU · MURPHY, CHODOS + AUF DER MAUR.

THE BOY FROM WESTMOUNT · BRIAN GALLERY/CONRAD BLACK.

LIES! · BILL FOX

LITTLE BRO by OLIVE · PEGGY.

BIG BRO by DOREEN, Gary + Barbara.

MY SON THE TRUCKER · IRENE MULRONEY.

BRIAN + I · PETER C. NEWMAN.

A HISTORY of the POLKADOT by MILA

BEDTIME for BRIAN · REAGAN

MY COUNTRY FOR A MANDIBLE · J. CLARK

DITTO · M. McTEER

WE CAN'T BELIEVE WE ATE THE WHOLE THING! · Press Gallery

BONES BEFORE TAB · N. RAYMOND

HOW WE DID IT! · FOTHERINGHAM

WHERE I STOOD · BRIAN

Will This Smiling Never End?

The Mulroney show moved to Ottawa with Mila and one Giovanni Mowinckel taking batting practice on Stornoway before the big game at 24 Sussex Drive. Checks and polka dots — all so *très, très,* not yet *trop, trop.*

Trudeau finally stepped down, but what was wrong with Turner? He looked and sounded like he had some mysterious internal disorder. Maybe he did: he called a summer election campaign.

Canadians are intensely political, but only when wearing tuques. Like the rest, I passed on politics and went on vacation. When I returned, Brian Mulroney was the new PM, as we knew he would be.

211 Little Pigs Went to Market

September 4, 1984. Canadians send 211 Tories to Ottawa, the largest majority in Canadian history. And Bones had increased the PC representation in Quebec from one seat to fifty-eight! Who were these people?

Safe to say the Tories were going to be unbearable — until they screwed up.

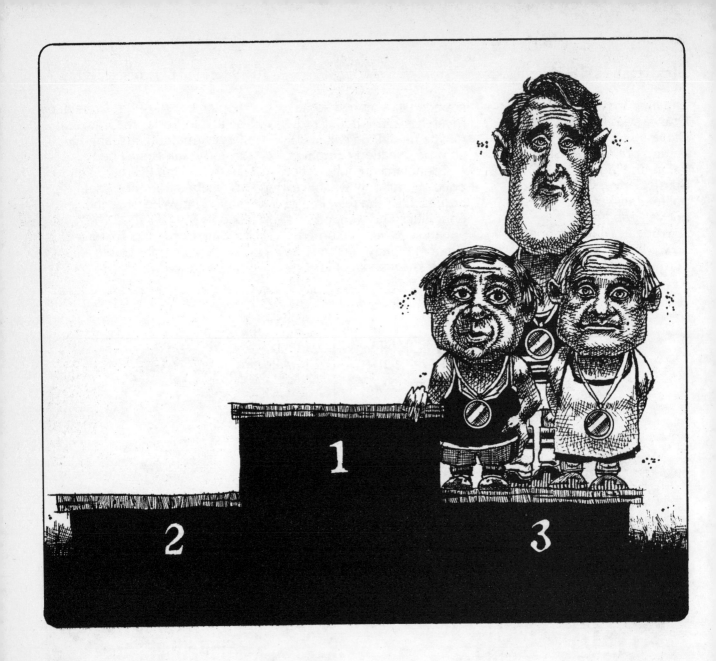

There were great flurries of political activity — smiling premiers, peace-pipes offered to native leaders, economic summits announced, offshore agreements signed. All this optimism was making me queasy, particularly when Patrick MacAdam called from the PMO.

"Hi, Terry!"

Did I know this guy? Were we long-lost drinking buddies? It sure sounded like it.

MacAdam was putting together a book of cartoons to present to the PM. Would I do one? Top dollar, of course.

One thing about the Tories, they generally have a better sense of humour and a thicker hide than the Liberals or NDPers. I suppose it's a sign of having arrived when a politician is recognizable enough to appear in an editorial-page cartoon. (Executive assistants have sometimes sent letters wondering why I haven't drawn the boss yet.)

Tories also tend to pay well for an original cartoon. Liberals and NDPers are usually cheap, often trying to wheedle drawings for nothing as if I should be flattered by the request.

"Oh, you actually want money?"

"A-one. And preferably in cash so none of you crapheads in Ottawa get any of it back."

Only Tories laugh at that line. But then, they can usually afford to.

How Long?

But, when were the Tories going to trip over their inexperience like any decent new government should? True, Cabinet minister Bob Coates made a murky visit to a striptease club in West Germany, but his resignation was swift and decisive. And Solicitor General Elmer MacKay did meet privately with Richard Hatfield to discuss the possiblity of pot-possession charges being laid against the fun-lovin' New Brunswick premier.

But these were only minor dust-ups.

There were signs of hope when Michael Wilson's first budget proposed limits on old-age pension increases. Grey power mobilized. Bones was confronted on the front steps of Parliament by one Solange Denis, who accused him of lying and called him "Charlie Brown."

But then the proposal was dropped, and Brian admitted that the government had been wrong.

Wrong? What? Was this the same Bones who used to fire off four-page letters to the editor if his name was spelled incorrectly? Was Brian learning humility?

I began to panic.

Other cartoon sources were

NEWS ITEM: MORE DEMANDS THAT HATFIELD RESIGN.

36

also drying up before my eyes. Robert Bourassa was being premier of Quebec again, so quietly that he didn't inspire a *Gazette* cartoon for eighteen months.

It was a logical time for any sane cartoonist to turn to drink. I sobered up instead. Was it making me paranoid? I believe in the freedom to change, but one media type, who used to preach that we'd have to shoot all the capitalist dogs, hired a financial analyst to advise him on his portfolio.

Nancy Southam, of — yes — that family, had always seemed one of the guys, being a baseball fanatic and all. But suddenly she started chumming it up with Mila Mulroney and throwing Let's Get to Know the Tories parties for misguided Montrealers.

Mordecai Richler would be in one corner being chatted up by Finlay MacDonald while Nick Auf der Maur would be in another telling Dalton Camp elephant jokes. Allan Fotheringham and Richard Hatfield chug-a-lugged B.C. wine out on the balcony, and Peter C. Newman seemed to be hitting on Conrad Black for investment tips. L. Ian MacDonald was signing copies of his Bones-approved biography before it could be remaindered.

But no, I wasn't paranoid: they *were* out to get me. Personally. Brian was on the telephone, calling Carol and me to wish us a happy wedding anniversary. *Oh joy*. Then my father received a personalized letter from Mulroney, wishing him well on his eightieth birthday. (The signature was done with a rubber stamp.) Dad, God bless him, threw the letter away — still grumpy about those Whigs after all these years.

All this attention was becoming a major-league worry. Was I was being courted as official court jester to the Progressive Conservative Party of Canada, fer crissakes? Was I doomed for life to joke it up with Brian's then best friends, Michel Cogger and Brian Gallery, at Whiff of Grape dinners?

Perhaps a new career was called for. I could draw nice *He shoots! He scores!!!* cartoons of smiling hockey players for Les Canadiens? Forget it. Ronald Corey, the Habs' president, was another of Brian's best friends.

Who could I turn to? Nick Auf der Maur and I had once planned to attack the U.S. embassy in Ottawa during a Richard Nixon visit. We'd bomb it with plastic bags filled with macaroni and ketchup, Nixon's favourite meal. We'd use a helicopter flown by a Vietnam vet. But helicopters turned out to be expensive and, well, the idea was scuttled. But, hey, it's the thought that counts.

Now, here was Nick, asking Mulroney favours. During the Shamrock Summit in Quebec City, would Brian and Reagan sign a birthday card for Nick's daughter Melissa?

They did. It was on the front page of *The Gazette*. Aaaargh.

The moment of truth came when Bob McCready, a stalwart in the composing room at *The Gazette*, accosted me on the elevator. "How come you're not doing to Mulroney what you used to do to Trudeau? Have you lost it?"

Maybe I had.

But Black September was approaching, and I would get my spitball back. Within months, I could do a reality check with Bob: "How'm I doing?"

"Fine, just fine." Bob was suddenly smiling.

Black September Saves My Butt

One year after the election, the Tory honeymoon was over and, to the delight of all muckrakers, it's been a rocky relationship ever since.

CBC's "fifth estate" kicked things off with their report on a million cans of tainted tuna being released on an unsuspecting public, after

EUROPE ON $1,000.⁰⁰ A DAY WITH SUZANNE BLAIS-GRENIER...

C'EST FUN!

Richard Hatfield convinced about-to-be-fired Fisheries minister John Fraser to save some four hundred jobs at the New Brunswick tuna plant.

The best part of the scandal was that we got our first glimpse of Mulroney's true nature. First, several days of heated posturing; then Fraser was humiliated and callously fired. Attractive man, Bones.

Finally, in an interview with *The New York Times*, Mulroney revealed that his recollection of the Tuna Derby also smelled. We have been sniffing the fumes from his childlike ability to recall himself in a flattering light ever since. Bones himself has no sense of smell at all. Lucky for him.

As each new scandal erupted, ever shallower depths of Brian were revealed. After Chris Young of Southam News reported that Environment minister Suzanne Blais-Grenier had wasted $65,000 on two chauffeur-driven trips

around Europe, the media focused on how inept she was in her portfolio. Her days were numbered, but not before Brian suggested to the French media that the pursuit of Blais-Grenier was racist.

But the media could flush out English-Canadian cabinet ministers too, and they would prove as unattractive as anything Quebec had to offer.

The Globe and Mail initially raised questions about suspicious dealings between Sinc Stevens and a Korean bank. This led to revelations of complicated deals involving Stevens's wife, Noreen, in which money was raised for supposedly dormant companies. Mulroney's shrill insistence on his belief in Stevens's virginal innocence merely led sensible people to assume that Sinc was godfather to the Mulroneys' children.

Luckily, the Liberal Rat Pack proved to be almost as embarrassingly shrill as the Tories. When the House of Commons was looking a lot like a playpen, Mulroney suggested that what the media and opposition were up to was … no, not Watergate, but McCarthyism! By the time an inquiry had finally found Sinc guilty, and the taxpayers shelled out for his huge legal fees, we had also bought some comic relief in Sinc's Christ-

NEWS ITEM: BLAIS-GRENIER FINALLY QUITS CABINET...

HI, NOREEN. HOW'VE YOU BEEN?
...NO, IT'S SINC...SINCLAIR STEVENS,
YOUR HUSBAND!! SAY, I WAS JUST
READING WHERE YOU BORROWED
$2.6 MILLION—CONGRATULATIONS!
BUT, LISTEN, I WAS WONDERING—
WITH INCOME TAX AND ALL—IF YOU
COULD SPOT ME $50. UNTIL THE
END OF THE MONTH?...NO, HUH?

coin cottage industry.

Now I go into this in some detail because, I must admit, Sinclair Stevens is not my favourite person. When I was growing up, there were a lot of men in Toronto who seemed to come from a similar mold: glib, self-satisfied for no discernible reason — Foster Hewitt types with pork-pie hats who told big-tit and Jewish jokes. Their world had room for only Toronto, *The Tely*, and the cottage. Anyway, Sinclair Stevens pushed all those buttons. Was I being fair? Who cares. From then on, anything the Tories did was fair game.

Now, before you go all politically correct on me, the Toronto type that I didn't like had his equivalent in Montreal: a loud glad-hander who always knew his way around. The Montreal type was Union Nationale.

Both these types seemed to have a magnetic attraction to Bones. First, Michel Gravel, a Tory MP from Montreal, was charged with fifty counts of influence peddling. *Fifty*.

The first few scandals in the Quebec Conservative caucus, Mulroney's heart and soul, created a feeding frenzy in the

FEATURING SOME of SINC'S I·N·F·A·M·O·U·S ROUTINES!!

CHRIST COIN TRICKS
★ ★ ★ ★ ★ ★ ★ ★
KITING BIG CHEQUES
★ ★ ★ ★ ★ ★ ★ ★
PAY MY LAWYERS AND I PROMISE NOT TO SQUEAL
★ ★ ★ ★ ★ ★ ★ ★
WHAT'S 2 MILLION?
★ ★ ★ ★ ★ ★ ★ ★
HOW TO MILK A BEAVER

 PORKY MULDOON PRODUCTIONS PROUDLY PRESENTS

ADDITIONAL ACTS

MILA AND THE HOLT-RENFREWETTES
★ ★ ★ ★ ★ ★ ★
ROCH AND ROLL
★ ★ ★ ★ ★ ★ ★
WILD CAGED TUNA
★ ★ ★ ★ ★ ★ ★
COATES BOTTOMLESS
★ ★ ★ ★ ★ ★ ★
SUZANNE'S LIMO HIGH WIRE ACT
★ ★ ★ ★ ★ ★ ★
BISSONNETTE'S B.B.Q. CHICKENS

THE $INC $TEVENS CIRCUS!

MERCIFULLY CANCELLED

"LET'S FACE IT, THERE'S NO WHORE LIKE AN OLD WHORE." BRIAN MULRONEY~JULY 14, 1984.

MS. FEBRUARY.

TORY OF THE MONTH.

BRIAN'S CABINET TURKEY SHOOT

SIGH...

PRESS

Suzanne Blais-Grenier
Robert Coates
Roch Lasalle
André Bissonnette
Sinclair Stevens
Michel Coté
Michel Gravel
Sondra Gotlieb
Michel Gratton
Simon Reisman

Edouard Desrosiers
Jean-Luc Joncas
Ronald Reagan
Gabriel Fontaine
_____ard Grisé
___n Gallery
___chel Cogger
___cien Bouchard
___hard Hatfield
___ Buchanan

"THE PRESS GETS IT WRONG. AGAIN. THE DALAI LAMA REFUSES TO SEE ME."

English media. And a majority of the first-term scandals involved Quebec members. Some, like Gravel, headed for the trough with a shovel. Others merely had better table manners.

Another head rolled courtesy of my colleague Claude Arpin of *The Gazette*. (Claude, long a fellow Mulroney watcher, had been wooed by Brian but demurred to fight another day.) Arpin exposed a scam involving junior Transport minister André Bissonnette and land flips of property outside Montreal to be used by Oerlikon Aerospace. Bissonnette was fired, and eventually charged with fraud and conspiracy.

Listing the scandals that followed would tax your patience and my good humour, so I've simply scattered relevant cartoons throughout the rest of this book. It seems cabinet ministers and Brian's best friends would just keep on being implicated. (Lately we've even been able to make side bets on the effect of scandals on the international money markets.)

And somewhere along the line my interest in Brian Mulroney became, well, almost compulsive.

Moving right along to ABORTION...

A Growing Obsession: Brian's Body Language

After drawing non-stop for four or five hours, my hand, or whatever possesses it, seems to take over the process and starts coming up with far better ideas and renderings than I ever could. When this happens I just sit back and watch.

After Mulroney had been around for several years, strange things began to happen to me during these intense drawing sessions: I began to see Mulroney-type features in inanimate objects: in a light bulb, in the pumpkin's face at Hallowe'en, etc.

The plasticity of marshmallows led me inexorably to the Pillsbury Doughboy — and Brian. Shadowed suggestions of his facial contours were there in my sandwich bread: three dimples — his closely set eyes and the scar on his forehead just above his nose.

On my dentist's office wall is an illustrated chart of the progression of tooth decay. How was it possible that no one else saw Bones in it? Obviously, I was obsessed.

At first, I just doodled. Then, as an exercise, I would see if I could incorporate Mulroney's

The Lambada!!! The latest sexy dance craze ...

...AND I'VE GOT THIS REAL COOL PAD UP ON MEECH LAKE...

physiognomy into random objects. I could suddenly picture how Jim Henson might do Brian up as a Muppet. I noticed that Planters were trying to revive Mr. Peanut and — yes!

This evolving artform took on a life of its own. To feed my madness, the real Brian, up there in Ottawa, just had to say something — not even anything of interest, such as: "Mr. Speaker! The fine, upstanding gentleman in question — So-and-so, the Honourable Member for Blah-blah-blah — is a great and honourable bagman, and my best friend!"

H-m-m-m … Brian is obviously lying again. Honourable, eh? Lyin' Brian. Draw him as a lion? Nobody'll

ROTTEN TOOTH

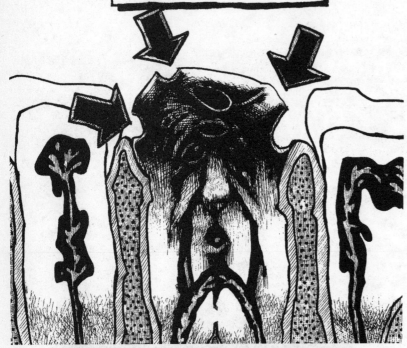

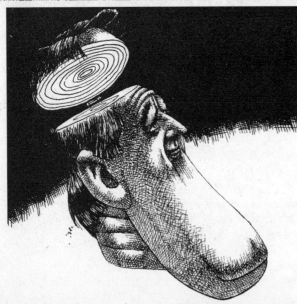

A Carp

get it, except perhaps some historian down the road. So what?

Shakes and shingles are in the news. *Say, that's softwood, isn't it?*

"I'll bet you can't make him look like a tree stump," my new demon challenged.
"I'll bet I can," I responded. And did.

At a festive family affair, I was even less talkative than usual. I was busy, engaged in an animated conversation with my fixation. *"Look at that ham, sitting there in the middle of the table."*
"Yeah. So?"
"Who's the biggest ham in Canada?" it asked me craftily.
"You're right. There he is again. Thanks!"
"Any time, pal."

This whole thing was becoming arcane. *"For this morning's sketching exercise,"* — this new friend was now inhabiting my inner ear — *"we draw Brian Mulroney as — ta-dah! — a carp!."*
"Not just a fish?" I ask.
"No. It has to be a carp. A big minnow really, blah, greyish, sluggish — a bottom dweller. Overweight — it eats the other fishes' garbage."

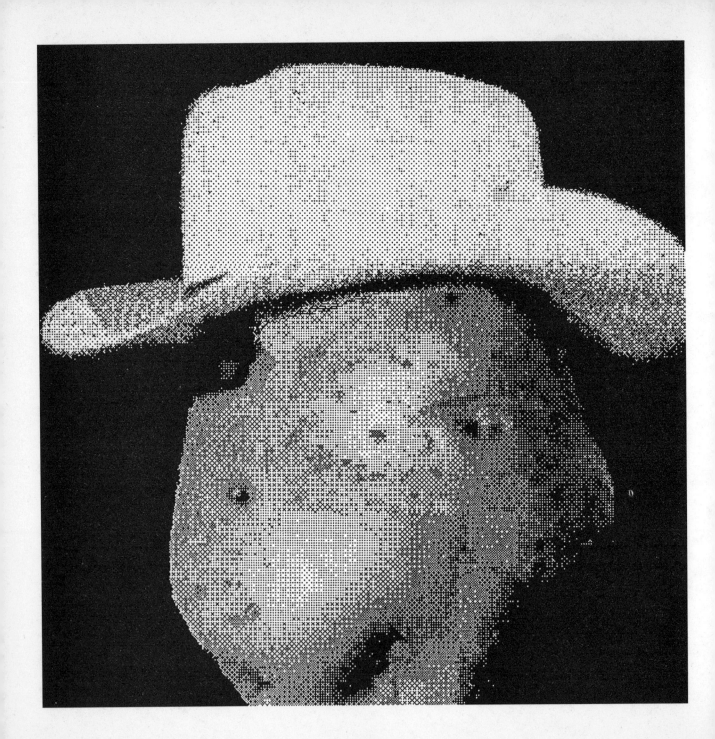

"Any other angle?" I wondered.

"*If you insist on puns, how about a 'carper,' someone who complains a lot, who finds fault with everyone else.*"

"Very clever," I observed. "But do you mind if I finish reading the box scores first?"

"*No problem!*" it said. "*How'd HoJo do last night against the Padres?*"

I was about to toss a grocery store's newspaper insert at him, but there Brian was again — right there, in that potato. I charged around *The Gazette* newsroom, pointing out my latest discovery. The inmates seemed baffled. So I scanned the photo of the potato into my computer and, to clarify that it was Brian in profile, I added a cowboy hat. This was cheating, of course — not making Bones look like a spud, but putting a hat on him. Brian never wears hats. He can't. He has a size nine head, rare as an Irish Tory.

The Gazette printed the spud caricature, but looked at me strangely.

For anyone but a cartoonist, such an obsession would probably be thought of as — well — unhealthy: mass murderers, I'm told, jump-start their careers this way. But cartoons are a great safety valve. Drawing them allows us to be okay the rest of the time. After the act, we're nice people.

I seem to have passed through the worst of my obsession, and my editors look quite relieved; but they still won't let *The Gazette* nurse take me off the Lithium.

Unfortunate Body Language

What had happened to me was not unique. As Canadians got to know Brian Mulroney, they began to respond — badly — to his body language.

Mulroney really learned to speak French well at Laval University in the 1960s; but his body language is much better received when his audience is French. Many Quebeckers are genuinely puzzled by English Canadians' revulsion. (This may explain why the French caricaturists aren't all that tough on Bones.)

On the other hand, English Canada finds Jean Chrétien passionately patriotic, charmingly French, and very humorous. In Quebec, cartoonists — and, indeed the rest of the media — go absolutely berserk whenever his name is mentioned. To some extent, this is a reaction to his old-fashioned federalist policies, but how much is it a base reaction to how he looks? Would Quebeckers want themselves pictured around the world as Jean Chrétien, Prime Minister?

Take another example: Brian Mulroney is generally not trusted or liked, even by many of the Canadians who hold their noses and vote for him. Don Mazankowski, however, *is* well liked. He has enemies, as

TODAY, THE COUNTRY WAS STRONG, FIRM, VIRILE...AND I WAS O.K. TOO...

⇨WHILE IT IS TRUE THAT QUEBEC'S PURE LAINE PRESS' HASN'T BAGGED A CABINET MINISTER, OR ANYONE ELSE OF IMPORTANCE, THEY DO SEEM A SOPHISTICATED LOT, UNTIL...

...JEAN CHRETIEN'S NAME COMES UP.

any competent politician must, but even a fair number of Liberals are genuinely fond of good old Maz. Yet he is a Mulroney adviser and a member of the same government, and preaches exactly the same policies.

So, what's the difference? Is it what Mulroney says? No, it's how he says it. In this era of TV politics, appearance, style, and charisma are often more important than political substance or minimal intelligence.

In a genuine world, we would judge leaders by what they promise and later accomplish. A century ago, Brian Mulroney would have been a fine prime minister, maybe even a progressive one. His style — gregarious and personal — is perfectly suited to a time when politicians worked small, live crowds, when exaggeration and lies were easier to get away with, and even expected.

A century ago, voters (all men, of course) would have responded to him according to loyalty, patronage, and family voting traditions. The voters might see the prime minister on the hustings once every five or ten years. Not every night, close up, on "The National."

Few cartoonists claim any textbook knowledge of body language, but we seem to use it instinctively to transmit personality and emotion. Similarly, very few readers claim to be conscious of body language; yet we tell the world all about ourselves and respond to other people through messages sent out by our body movements.

Experts who *do* know the basics of body language will tell you that it is extremely difficult to change our mannerisms for more than a short period of time. The truth will out. Tell someone that you know a fair amount about body language and he or she will squirm, trying not to give anything away. After a few minutes, posing will be forgotten and his or her body will tell much, once again.

We live in a world in which words are overrated. We can sue people for what they say, but not for what they inflict on us through their body language. Yet, our reaction to others, including politicians, is usually quite base and primal.

Democracy is superior to other political systems. But how much better would it be if we didn't have women who won't vote for a man because he doesn't clip his nostril hairs?

Immediately after the John Turner – Brian Mulroney debate during the 1988 election, Canadians felt an overwhelming, if temporary, identification with John Turner. He telegraphed sincerity, passion, and drive. Brian looked like he'd just been caught with a hand in the cookie jar.

But can anyone remember what either man said?

Ronald Reagan's body language helped me re-evaluate my style of cartooning. I'd been drawing large heads, emphasizing the caricature, with bodies added almost as an afterthought. I was portraying Reagan as some big-headed evil Darth Vader type. It wasn't working.

But once I gave him big stuffed shoulders, and stuck a smaller, senile-looking, often lopsided head on top, the drawing became far more like him. In his second term, I began to age him like a prune, and greyed out one eye, suggesting a blind but still happy guy.

As the first real TV president, Reagan got me thinking about how we look at people. Usually we look at another person's face for no more than a few seconds at a time if he or she is looking back. Yet, on average, we watch TV for more than twenty hours a week. In fact, TV is how we look at people most often — head and shoulders. Knowing they're not looking back makes it comfortable.

Therefore, I squared the borders of my cartoons to more of a TV shape and allowed for plenty of surrounding white space, to draw the eye to what I wanted to express in the highly detailed front view of the face. Drawing profiles is much less work, but I usually draw caricatures that face the reader just like Peter Mansbridge does. We relate to eye contact, particularly if it isn't real.

In truth, we are comfortable looking at, and even studying, people in this TV-style format. When we take snapshots of one another, they are general, frontal shots or head and shoulders. Newspaper and magazine photographers have us look at people this way, too. So it made sense to bring this familiarity into my presentation of cartoons.

MacCartooning

All a cartoonist really needs is pen, paper, ink, and a little imagination. But the new technology is in evidence everywhere in today's newspaper world. So, several years ago, I began playing with a Macintosh computer and various graphic programs. And I now will sometimes draw complete cartoons or parts of them on the computer.

Other technologies are also useful. Take, for example, the photocopier. A photocopy of a photograph highlights details and features. It uglies people up; then I can ugly them up even more.

Look at this example of a Mulroney head.

Photocopies can show something else, too. If the lighting in the photograph is right, when you make a copy of a copy of a copy, it ages the person in the photo. Want to know what you might look like in twenty years? Give it a try.

With the aid of a photocopier and some knowledge of anatomy and how muscles sag, this is how I predict Brian will look one day. Mind you, that won't be for quite some time. Five years, perhaps.

A photocopy gives me visual shorthand, which is much more useful than the actual photo. Looking at the photocopy, in a few simple strokes I can do an initial rough sketch, emphasizing some things and ignoring others.

Clothes Make or Break the Man

Besides a good dictionary, my essential books consist primarily of references on how things look — How many tines are there in a standard fork, anyway? — and how people walk, talk, and communicate. An indispensable little volume is *Class* by American oddball Paul Fussell. It is a theory of how North Americans telegraph their social positions through what they eat, wear, and so on. (Fussell holds that television sets are a dead giveaway every time. The bigger and more prominent they are in our personal environment, the lower our class.)

Fussell claims that "Reagan violates virtually every canon of upper-class or even upper-middle-class presentation." Ronald Reagan and Brian Mulroney both dress like new money, too crisply groomed. The shirt collars are too white and starchy. Their ties are expensive and tell us so. Their suits are *always* buttoned, defensively. Denied the use of his pants pockets, there's nowhere for Mulroney's chubby little hands to go. His arms hang by his sides, looking dead.

In one of my favourite photographs of Mulroney, he is

WHAT ABOUT MY HANDS?

walking through Expo 67 with his then best friend Robert Stanfield. As usual, Stanfield's appearance is unobvious, old money (like George Bush). But Brian is wearing an off-the-wrong-rack, too-tight suit. And all three suit buttons (three being the style then) are buttoned.

The Mouth from Hell

Even worse than his taste in clothes is Mulroney's mouth. Physically, it is odd. (Roy Peterson, the cartoonist at *The Vancouver Sun*, once said jokingly that Mulroney didn't really have a such a big chin, just a very small mouth and no neck.) But the physical peculiarity isn't the problem: Brian just can't keep a zip on it.

When feeling in control of a situation, Brian can be really quite engaging. But then things start to fall apart. First, he starts to blow his own horn, then to exaggerate something to make a point. Next, he'll hammer the point home by lying like hell. Finally, beside himself at being caught out, he'll deny it all. Angered or frustrated, he goes into Righteous Indignation mode, glorious to see.

For serious people, such childishness is troubling; but for cartoonists it is the raw comic material of a magnificent obsession.

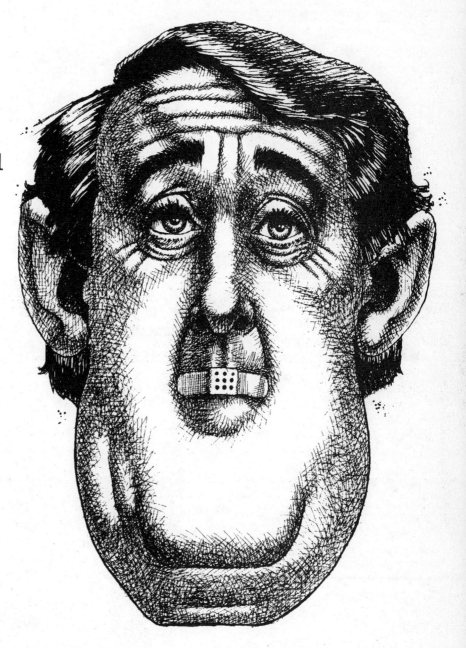

HOW THE IMAGE-MAKERS MIGHT INCREASE MULDOONEY'S APPEAL AMONGST WOMEN...

...OR YOU MIGHT CLEVERLY REFER TO THE OPPOSITION AS DEPLORABLE AND DISORIENTATED DIPSOMANIACS, SIR... NOT RAT KA-KA...

Should Mila Just Leave Him at Home?

Some politicians are really very nice people, I'm told. They give to charities, are loving parents, and cry at weddings. I'd rather not know this. Why run the risk of getting to like them? Why become fond of people who are involved in decisions that can profoundly affect our lives? A simple vote in the House of Commons creates new jobs and, these days, scraps old ones. And my job — that of any satirist — is to mock them, jeer, goad and test them and the system.

As Ed Broadbent put it, "The right to mock must be protected, for it is directly related to the idea of respect, respect for certain values which are seen to be absent in the subject held up to ridicule."

Humour comes easiest at the expense of others, hardest when directed at a cause for which we have personal sympathy. For example, it is hard for me to be as raucous when cartooning native peoples' concerns as when going after the Tories. Similarly, women are making strides, but still have genuine problems. In the public

"I WONDER HOW THE PRESS WOULD REACT IF I SUDDENLY DASHED OFF TO REGINA WITH TOMMY HUNTER?"

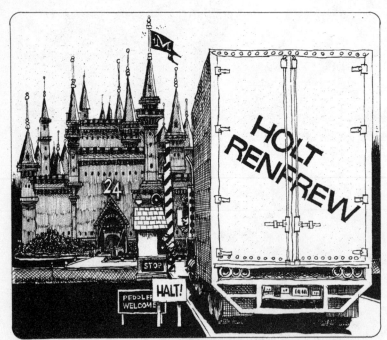

"I'VE GOT ANOTHER LOAD OF SHOES AND CLOTHES FOR IMELDA MULDOON."

debate, some feminists remind me of the self-righteous and shrill high-school teachers who taught me in the 1950s. However I can't draw them like this. It just doesn't feel right yet.

So I'm all for women gaining absolutely equal status, so I can mock them as I mock everybody else. Hurry it along, sisters.

Now, partners of politicians, that's tricky. They are constantly on public display and being trotted about on international visits. So they are fair game, but in a qualified way: they weren't elected, and didn't create the policies.

Margaret Trudeau had personal problems; but the press corps in Ottawa, to their credit, left her alone. It was only when the international media broke the Maggie – Rolling Stones story that Canadian papers grudgingly got on the roller-coaster.

When the story broke, I tried to keep to the politics, and drew this cartoon of Joe Clark and Maureen McTeer mulling over the events at the breakfast table.

Maureen McTeer was fair game, on a slow day, because she was always voicing opinions on political matters.

Which brings us to Mila Mulroney. Even Brian jokes about her habitual shopping sprees, and her office and staff

in the PMO costs taxpayers money, although no one seems to be able to find out how much. Moreover, because Brian flaunts Mila as the ultimate trophy wife and fashion accessory, it's sometimes tempting to be far tougher on her than she might deserve.

Yet, Brian also claims she is his best friend and adviser, which begs for our scrutiny. There is the suspicion that, left to his own devices, Brian would probably sport polyester suits and "sharp" white Créditiste shoes.

These would be the perfect complement to his ability to attract international gaffes: Brian goes to Washington, and Sondra Gotlieb slaps him off the front page; Brian goes to Africa, and the Oerlikon scandal breaks out at home; Brian's entourage detours into London only for a photo-op; Brian goes to Tokyo only, it seems, to confront Ontario socialists.

Mila may be young, but she seems to be an old-fashioned, pampered gal. But then, Brian's attitude towards women seems old-fashioned gallant, with a tendency to pamper, which is even more offensive. To give her credit, Mila's elegance does work well for Brian, and Canada, in the old-fashioned glitter of international diplomacy. I've

sometimes thought that Mila should just leave Brian at home.

True, Bones *is* learning — there are fewer public international embarrassments. But Brian Mulroney has been a disaster for Canada's image abroad. He craves the international standing of a Trudeau. ("One thing about the old Trud," Bones has said, "he's got a lotta class.") This he will never have.

*MRS. GOTLIEB'S WARDROBE COURTESY OF CANADIAN TIRE.

Brian Mulroney and his classy best friend, Mila, hosted the leaders of the Western world at an economic summit in Toronto. In attendance was his best friend Ronald Reagan and his best friend Margaret Thatcher. Muldoon's hundreds of best friends back in Baie-Comeau, Westmount, and Outremont were unable to attend. Mainly, it was a large photo-op, although the city did run up the attendees' national flags along University Avenue: the American and German flags tied for most paranoia-inducing.

Brian is such a suck. What's a cartoonist to do?

Canadians 'Я' Us and Free Trade

In the summer, political activity slows down, which is just as well, as I'm an avid baseball fan. During what's usually still winter I go to Florida for a couple of weeks to watch Spring Training. I listen to a lot of Jazz and some C & W on holidays on the south coast of Maine.

All these things are antidotes to my work — and all are American. So I'm not your typical screaming anti-American agitator. I have the usual middle-class Canadian attitudes about the United States. But I am aware that, if I want to remain Canadian, someone has to be strong and make rules to keep me from eating too much tempting stuff from the American candy store.

We've always had strong leaders who not only held Americans at arm's length, but also pulled Canadians back from temptation. But, today, the problem is this: Brian's working behind the counter.

For over a hundred years, many Montrealers have spent summer holidays in Maine. It's quiet and closer than the Maritimes. Maine

79

visiting George for lobster and photo-ops. On my way into town one morning, I came upon the brand-new heliport that Bush has had installed. And there, hovering above me, was this big helicopter. Then I realized: Brian Mulroney was leaving!

Insanely — just for a moment — a Bruce Cockburn song came to me: "If I had a rocket launcher."

Headline: CARTOONIST BLOWS UP MULDOON!!!

Crowds on beach cheer maniac on!

But... who'd pay my mortgage?

Brian Sings

The differences between North Americans are quite minimal. Does this explain why we cherish them so much?

Canadians, myself included, are such lazy dolts that, given the choice, we'll travel the American way every time. We're weak, dishevelled, fragile, and desperately seek American approval.

ANDRÉ PHILIPPE GAGNON ON THE JOHNNY CARSON SHOW!, screams a headline in *Le Journal de Montréal*. We'll report on how the three or four Canadian players in major league baseball are doing. Have they learned to chew tobacco and

would go bankrupt without Canadian summer dollars. Montrealers can always be found sitting on the beach, talking heatedly about Canadian politics, even when

George Bush is just a few miles down the road in Kennebunkport, out-jogging his Secret Service men.

A couple of summers ago, Brian Mulroney was

VERY CLEVER BRIAN!!

say stupid things, just like the pros do?

Ashamed of our collective insecurity, we're vulnerable and awkward in the face of the Americans. But we're towers of strength and confidence compared to Brian Mulroney.

Little Bones sang for the American bosses in Baie-Comeau and grew up to close down Schefferville, Quebec, for Iron Ore, the American company that made him rich. Brian's never stopped trying to please the Yanks. Having sold himself, he's now selling the rest of us so he can watch the All-Star game with his best friend George Bush.

In September 1985, Brian Mulroney gave in to temptation and sang the free-trade song to American applause. I was bemused but reminded of more passionate political times. The last attempt at establishing a free-trade pact with the United States, in 1911 or thereabouts, had spawned full-page newspaper cartoons hysterically for or against the concept of closer trade ties with the Yankees. Imagery reflected the sentimental morality of the time — distressed fair damsels threatened by fat, leering American men with terrible teeth. Free trade hadn't passed in 1911 and seemed unrealistic in 1985.

My rule of thumb in cartooning is this: If I don't understand an issue, the public probably doesn't either. I play it safe. I'm against it, whatever it is, until I understand it.

Initially, that's how I handled the slow-growing free-trade issue. At first, on a slow day, "The Dangers of Free Trade" made a passable subject for a cartoon, even though I thought nothing would come of it. Our society has become far too cumbersome to institute such far-reaching changes, I figured. Besides, they wouldn't get away with it, would they? Most Canadians would vote against it, wouldn't they?

Well, I got one thing right: more of us voted against it than for it; but Brian Mulroney still got the deal for his real best friends, the Americans.

Taking Sides

In theory, reporters should be fair, balanced, and neutral. Columnists are expected to be opinionated, but balanced, if not neutral. Editorial writers have to be balanced and fair, yet opinionated in expressing their newspaper's official line. The only neutral thing about them is that their work is anonymous, so no one knows who they are. (Perhaps this explains why most editorial writers look in need of a little off-beat sex.)

And political cartoonists? They generally try to be even-handedly unfair and off-balance — and to meet their deadlines. Ethics? They'd have to look it up in the dictionary.

Other newspaper people tend to leave cartoonists alone, like the village idiot. Therefore, cartoonists are rarely team players, refusing to embrace any cause, no matter how worthy.

As a rule this is no problem. But the free-trade question got to me. This was not just everyday, cynical irritation. I was really pissed off.

I'm no financial wizard. I never read the financial pages if I can help it. I'm not certain how many zeros there are in a billion — U.S. or Imperial — it's not one of my day-to-day problems.

As a fiscal idiot, I know I'm supposed to trust people who know these things. But, have you ever noticed how types who know about money never give it away? How you always end up in their offices, writing them cheques?

I DID IT THEIR WAY
Muldoon

GEORGE R. BELFRY the 3d. BLIND; HAS 15% HEARING IN ONE EAR; SPEAKS WITH A LISP; WORST DRESSED MAN OF THE PAST DECADE; LAST SEXUAL DALLIANCE IN 1948; EDITORIAL PAGE WRITER...LIBERAL.

What was really pissing me off was that (a) these guys were all cowabunga on free trade, and (b) none of them bothered to explain it in terms simple enough for me, and probably most other Canadians, to understand.

So I figured it out for myself: 10 + 1 = 11. Ten Yanks for every Canadian.

"Hey, no problem," the money guys laughed. "Trust us."

Should I trust a bunch of smiling guys wearing Michael Wilson glasses?

Every arrogant bank manager I'd ever had to deal with flashed through my mind. "Sure. Fuck you."

I found that I really, really wanted to do something more than just a few tart and punchy cartoons on an editorial page.

So I did.

ONE CANADIAN AND TEN AMERICAN BUSINESSMEN DISCUSS FREE TRADE...

... FRANKLY, FELLAS, SOME CANADIANS DON'T SEEM TO TRUST US!

Our "Comic Book"

Rick Salutin and I met just after the October Crisis in the early 1970s. He was in Montreal writing a piece on Quebec for *Harper's*. Rick is now a playwright, Toronto den-mother of Canadian nationalism, and a thorn in the side of many people in charge. Which is why I like him. People like Rick are rare these days. Salutin is also connected to the NDP/labour/feminist/literary crowd in Toronto, explaining what they're up to when I need to know.

Rick called me as the free-trade debate was picking up steam: Did I know a young cartoonist who might want to illustrate a comic book against The Deal?

As he explained how the text might work, I thought of cartoons I had drawn and others I had in mind that would work with each point he raised. Sensing my interest, he sent the rough text to me.

The manuscript was truly startling; but, was it all true? The left, like the right, has been known to exaggerate to make a point. So I took the text to Joan Fraser at *The Gazette*, who is very good at explaining tricky bits. Yes, she said, it was all *potentially* possible.

I then went to Mark Harrison, then editor at *The Gazette*, and explained what I wanted to do: make all my cartoons on free trade available for use, without charge, to any group fighting The Deal. Also, I wanted to let the cartoons be used free in a colour cartoon book, millions of copies of which would be distributed across the country. Many of the cartoons would be ones I had drawn for *The Gazette*.

I own the copyright on all my cartoons, so that wasn't a problem, but it was a sticky situation. Just this once, I wanted to take sides.

"Is that fair?" Mark asked.

"Well," I said. "If I draw any cartoons in favour of The Deal, then the pro–free trade groups can have them for nothing, too."

Mark smiled. "Okay. But just this once."

This was going to be very different from any book Rick or I had published. There was no money in it for either of us; but we both sensed that, if done right, this booklet might make a difference. Eighteenth-century pamphleteers must have felt like this, distributing political sheets illustrated with

Le libre-échange?
Parlons-en!

Quelques question~~s~~
simples et directes~~~~
le libre-é~~change~~

WHAT'S
THE BIG DEAL?

Some straightforward
questions and answers on
free trade.

cartoons in the dead of night.

Rick showed the roughs to groups in the Coalition Against Free Trade, and everyone was excited. To hell with the cost, they said. Let's get it out there.

The final text avoided all rhetoric. (Later, some learned group found that our booklet was the only publication on free trade — pro or con — that was understandable by someone without a university education; yet these were the very people who would be most hurt by free trade.)

Suddenly, a snag. The best cartoon in the booklet, *Two Great Canadians*, was found to be politically incorrect by a women's group in the Coalition: "No sisters are to be portrayed as hookers, notwithstanding our political determination to protect the rights of all female sex-industry workers...." That sort of thing.

I'm very bad at taking orders and, therefore, never do. (It's like drinking — if you're not good at it, don't do it.) However, after sleeping on it, I agreed to drop the cartoon (reproduced here). Getting on with things was more important.

Several million copies of the booklet were suddenly out there — being read, passed around, and read again. Within a week it was starting to do what we had hoped for — it was making a difference. Print could still work.

Television was reducing free trade to the usual "either/or and now a commercial." But our simple booklet was something people could read at their own pace, talk over, and think about. It gave them points to start asking questions about — and they were starting to ask. Barbara Frum and others began referring to "The Comic Book," and viewers knew what she was talking about. Both the Libs and the NDP were asking for as many copies as they could get for campaign literature.

(One night in *The Gazette* lobby, a staffer yelled, "You son of a bitch! You could stop The Deal with that god-damned silly little book of yours!"

"Do you really think so?" I asked, genuinely heartened.)

People in the Coalition had been worried that the booklet would come out too late; but, in fact, it was released too early. We had given the Business lobby time to respond. Very rapidly, the Business Coalition on National Issues (read, multinationals and wannabees) put together a newspaper insert in response to our booklet. It was released right on time, just before the election.

It cost them millions, I'm happy to say — their class of help wanted to be paid. They

even commissioned my pal Andy Donato, from *The Toronto Sun*, to draw cartoons for it. Andy was the logical choice. *The Sun* is a nutty, proudly right-wing newspaper where notorious Canadian characters go to write columns before they die. In the end, Andy's cartoons weren't used, but he got big bucks anyway, as he should.

Canadians who wouldn't have been caught dead together before found themselves side by side in the trenches, fighting against the free-trade deal. And they fought it to the fifteenth round, with the result that more people voted against The Deal than for it.

John Turner, whom many of us never had much time for, went out with his head held high — higher than it had been in his life.

The Fight didn't turn me into a raving politico, but Rick did introduce me to people and organizations who still cared about things other than money. Maude Barlow, the feisty head of The Council of Canadians, became a pal. So did her husband, Andrew Davis, who is much funnier and should give her a hand with her speeches. We all talk — about Canadian politics and other things — on the beach in Maine.

Joan Fraser at *The Gazette* wrote against The Deal. Her editorials, combined with my cartoons, forced our then publisher, Clark Davey, to write a signed front-page editorial in favour of free trade. Some saw this as ominous; but it was Clark's paper, and he could write what he wanted. He always let me draw what I wanted, even though my cartoons probably embarrassed him. I hope so, anyway.

The Edmonton Journal and *The Toronto Star* were the only Canadian newspapers to make a clear stand against free trade. They were astonishingly brave, given the pressures — from advertising to accessibility — that business can bring to bear on a newspaper. Edmonton's too far west, but I'm now working for John Honderich at *The Toronto Star* as a direct result of the free–trade fight. Indeed, Rick Salutin was a prime mover in getting me there.

I gained a lot from The Fight. After years of becoming a less caring, skeptical observer, I regained a hold on something I'd been losing: Canadianism. I'm still not a flag-waving fanatic, mind you; just a Canadian.

Itching for another Fight.

B&B: Brian and Bob

In 1976, after Brian Mulroney had lost his first run at the Tory leadership, the voters unceremoniously heaved Bourassa out. For a time he was the plague — but not to Brian Mulroney, who bought him lunch.

Not long after Mulroney won the Tory leadership, Bourassa was premier again. We don't know who bought lunch, but Bones and The Boo have set the political agenda for Quebec and Canada ever since. A new day was at hand. These guys were best friends.

Not like those two scorpions in a bottle, Trudeau and Lévesque.

And yet, today, the Quebec-Canada dialogue has never been worse. Go figure.

QuébéCan Inc.

Journalists are always travelling across Canada (by train, moped, or "Journal" van), doing magazine, newspaper, TV, or radio pieces. "If only Canadians could come to their senses and see what a beautiful country they have," these folks gush, "they wouldn't tear it apart!" Yawn.

Yes, it is a beautiful country, but we folk prefer donut shops to the Rockies. We don't want panoramas, we want to talk about what those Quebeckers are up to or the latest plot to destroy *mon pays* by *les autres.*

We may well be the silliest people on earth.

This is handy for us in the media who know that the Quebec-Canada story is the only thing that makes us interesting. So we aren't going to let it go.

It's also good for another small group, the Affluently Bilingual running the company stores: the Brian Mulroneys, Robert Bourassas, Jean Chrétiens, and Paul Martins in all fields.

QuébéCan is one major-league industry.

Bourassa claims to be neutral on the federal election

THE MEECH LAKE MONSTER

Take two average guys, one in Drummondville, Quebec, say, and the other in Prince Rupert, B.C. They wear the same clothes, live in similar houses, probably drive aging Hondas, and eat too much junk food. Their kids watch the same music videos, drink the same soft drinks, and wear high-tops. Both have to pay their Visa bills on time, one in French, the other in English.

The two men don't trust each other, and haven't since 1066. This is a good thing, at least for the media and the Affluently Bilingual.

Brian Mulroney promised to bring Quebec into the Canadian fold. Eleven men in suits walked into a room. Then they walked out again, saying they had a deal — it only had to be approved back home in the provinces. But the men in suits weren't paying close enough attention. They had forgotten about 1066.

An American friend — he runs a candy store — asked me to explain why Meech Lake had failed "in two words or less."

We've had these What-silliness-are-your-people-up-to-now? talks before.

"Distinct society," I said.

Light bulbs did not appear over his head, so I continued.

"Forget about the strategic stuff. It boiled down to two words: *distinct* and *society*. No

one, right up to the prime minister, could define to everyone's satisfaction what 'distinct society' would mean. Therefore, not one Canadian could understand what Meech Lake would mean.

"Nevertheless, most of the French population wanted Meech Lake because Bourassa told them they did. Most of the English population didn't want Meech Lake because they didn't trust Quebec to want Meech Lake. Then most Quebeckers were furious when they didn't get Meech Lake. And most of the English were happy that Meech Lake fell through because that had put Quebec in its place. Got that?"

My American pal looked vacant.

"So how's Tim Raines working out with the White Sox?" I asked.

Watching the premiers huddled for that last week of Meech–wrangling, I couldn't help feeling a certain perverse respect for Mulroney's determination to make this thing happen. And, the last night, with all the premiers singing "O Canada"— even Bourassa joining in, albeit hesitantly — I decided to be nice. I drew Mulroney pulling a hat out of a rabbit.

But then Clyde Wells walked out and I needed a substitute cartoon. My one nice caricature of Brian didn't get printed. So, here it is — how often do we get a second chance?

Lucky for us, Meech Lake coincided with the Berlin Wall coming down. (The Wall might have been a major event around the world, but, in Canada, it had to fight for headlines with Meech.) One of the suspicious aspects of the Berlin Wall story was people selling hunks of it — or any old piece of cement — as a chunk of history. So, what was to prevent Mulroney from selling suitable if not quite authentic souvenirs of Meech Lake?

Les Anglos sont là

Newspapers are looking more and more like insurance companies. The furious clackity-clack of typewriters is only a smoke-free memory, and an Underwood as hard to find as a Gitane. Only a major event brings back the action.

The night fourteen female engineering students at l'Université de Montréal were murdered, *The Gazette* was livelier than any time since the eve of the 1980 referendum. I rushed down to the paper to replace the cartoon I had done earlier in the day.

I drew two crying women comforting each other in the shadow of U. of M. tower, considered Montreal's most prominent phallic symbol. Whether the reference was understood by readers didn't matter, as long as the tower seemed ominous and threatening.

The Gazette is accused by some of being too protective of Anglos; others say it sells out the English by pandering to Quebec. Whatever the truth, *The Gazoo* does, at times, reflect Anglo paranoia.

The night of the shooting, the killer's identity was established just in time for the first edition. An editor then blurted out the fear that had been on many minds: "Thank

Leonard Cohen

God, the bastard wasn't English."

Anglos are tired of the wear-and-tear of an ongoing public discussion, debate, sometimes diatribe. Most are weary of the image of Anglos as kilted, unilingual, tweedy rose growers with gilt-framed portraits of Queen Victoria in their mansions.

It's a milkable myth. There are still a few rich ones, but they have little control in Quebec anymore. More Anglos are now on welfare than ever before.

By and large, Anglos are no longer categorizable. They now speak far more French than they used to, and some have completely integrated into the francophone milieu. (True, others sit poised for the flight from the West Island to Scarborough, Ontario — just in case.)

Jean-Pierre Girerd, the cartoonist at *La Presse,* once asked me to define an Anglo for him: he couldn't come up with a caricature prototype. The closest he came was to draw all English women with skinny, hairy legs.

Brian Mulroney started his climb up the political and financial ladder from the heart of Montreal's English establishment. He worked hard at being popular, and was rewarded by being made Grand Marshall of the 1980

WELCOME TO THE 90's...

St. Patrick's Day Parade. It's the largest Anglo bash of the year, and attracts half a million festive people.

But Mulroney became PM with the support of a heavily nationalist Quebec caucus. So, speaking up when Anglos are being maligned is now inappropriate, to use one of his favourite words. Mulroney is still seen at The Ritz on occasion. And Mila still shops at Holt-Renfrew and on Greene Avenue. But Brian can't show his face at the St. Patrick's Day Parade.

The English community of Montreal made Brian Mulroney. But today, there is no place where he is despised more.

Well, in eastern Canada, anyway.

HOW ABOUT A NEW COAT-of-ARMS FOR CANADA?

DEDICATED TO MAKING CTV LOOK RATIONAL

HONDA Century 21

VISA DUNKIN DONUT

From silly sea to the other silly sea

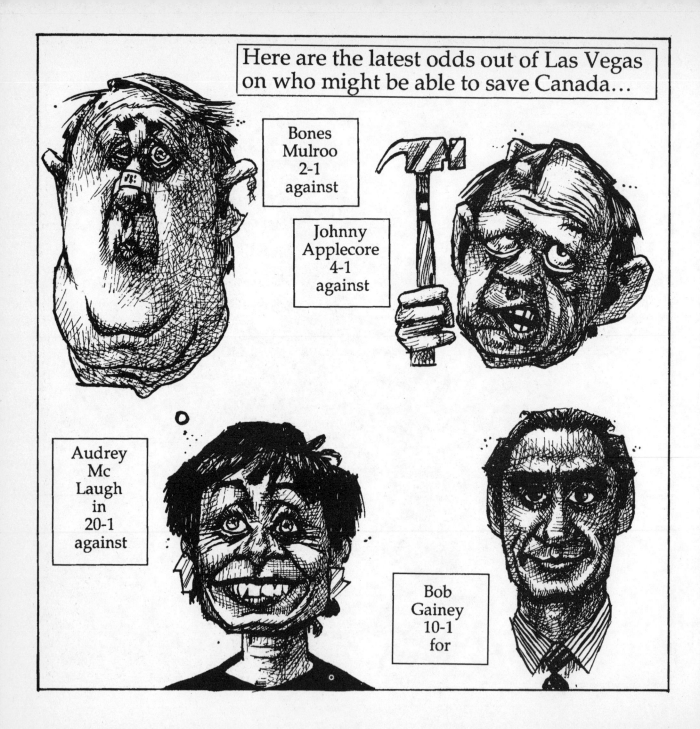

Here are the latest odds out of Las Vegas on who might be able to save Canada...

Bones Mulroo 2-1 against

Johnny Applecore 4-1 against

Audrey Mc Laugh in 20-1 against

Bob Gainey 10-1 for

Brian: The Sequel

Maclean's comes across my desk. The cover story proclaims, "The Private Prime Minister: An Exclusive Close-up of Brian Mulroney in Words and Pictures." Yep. Real private.

Will this be the Tory sell — Brian, the wounded but wiser warrior?

He's prepared for this feature with, I'd guess, a week's worth of Florida tanning. And, awww ..., doesn't he look comfortable, frolicking by the pool with his kids? And, yes! — his suit jacket is buttoned up. Thank goodness he's still getting bad advice.

HURRY, DOCTOR!!! THERE'S SOME EVIDENCE OF LIFE OVER HERE!

There's no doubt about it: Brian's reviving. Has he lost a bit of weight? Is Mila keeping him away from the cookie jar? Let's hope not. For months after the failure of Meech Lake, Muldoon's chins — no longer a visible jaw — were providing cartoonable new dimples and crevasses.

The phone rings. Michael Bate, head fiend at *Frank* magazine, wants to know if this silly book is finished, so I can get back to the more serious business of undermining Canada.

"Have you seen *Maclean's*?" Bate asks. He is toying with a send-up, a day in the life of Brian. Could I find photos of Hitler and Eva Braun to manipulate on the computer?

Frank is a rare bit of Canadian fresh air. It started out in Halifax several years ago but took on a life of its own when it expanded to Ottawa.

Rude, saucy, and produced on cheap newsprint, it thrives on the current Tory regime, and has deep-throats in every nook and cranny of the government and media. Most people I know read *Frank*, and many complain that the magazine gets things wrong; but when it arrives they all sit

down and read it cover to cover, the proof being in the pudding.

The publishers have no money, so it's pointless to sue them. Some of their sources are trying to settle a score, which encourages the victims to become sources in revenge.

Frank should have a rosy future, for Bones is at it again. The *Maclean's* article is the drumroll sounding the start of the Conservative march towards the next election.

And the Tories might well win at least a minority if the Liberals continue to flounder in Quebec under Jean Chrétien. And if Audrey McLaughlin remains, well, Audrey McLaughlin. And, of course, Brian has the goods on Lucien Bouchard. Brian is not clever. Brian can be a dolt. But Brian has more determination than anyone else. And more money.

Like *Frank*, "The Royal Canadian Air Farce," Laurier LaPierre, Erica Ehm — anyone involved in satire — I'd be pleased to have the wonder kid from Baie-Comeau around for another few years, never mind a populace so damned crazy — or is it now "intellectually disadvantaged" — that they would hang this albatross around the country's neck again.

FRANK BY NAME, FRANK BY NATURE

FRANK

$2.00

may 30, 1991
every two weeks
issue 90
central canada edition

MAKEUP!...

AISLIN '91
FRANK MAGAZINE

Hey kids?

Can you draw an egg?

And now a diamond?

Another smaller egg?

And a smaller upside-down diamond?

Great! That was the tough part. Now try some squiggles like these...

And now, some dots like, umm, holes. Do it by turning the brush.

A few rectangles...

A few triangles.

Now you're ready to draw:

Brian Mulroney, The Prime Minister of Canada!

READY, SET, GO! ...

**One egg ... now a second inside ... first diamond ...
second upside-down one ... four dots. Excellent.**

**And now, a flick-flick here and a flick-flick there. Here a flick, there a flick,
everywhere a flick-flick. Perfect.**

Draw two rectangle glasses, two diamonds for his tie, two more real big ones for his shoulders. Way to go, kids!

Two rectangles for his ears, fill in some black areas ...

... a few touch-ups with the pen,
and voilà!!! ...

Martin Brian Mulroney,
Prime Porker of Canada

CHILDREN! IGNORE THIS MANIAC!..
WE SHOULD'VE HAD HIM CASTRATED
YEARS AGO, WHEN WE HAD THE CHANCE, IN THE RAINBOW BAR + GRILL...

The Last Word — I Promise

There is safety in the bravado of youth, in not understanding what's going on or who's in charge. Nothing gets in the way of the assumption that you could do a better job.

In the early 1970s, we young people led the league in bravado. There was much talk of how revolutionary we were, although in truth we were only slightly risqué. The vanguard knew, too, that we would take over some day.

Now, in the early 1990s, we have done just that — in politics, finance, the media, and other fields that make a difference. And things are worse.

Canada is a less caring country than it should be, given the decent foundation handed to us. My children, their friends, and people like them are the first generation that assumes, probably rightly, things won't get much better, given the way we played fast and loose with Reaganomics and plain old greed all throughout the 1980s.

Today's newspapers are glossier but less substantial than they used to be, concerned less with scrutinizing and improving the system than with Cher's tattoos. Those competent people still in place are becoming very, very careful: Conrad Black's chill *is* a factor.

I'm fortunate. I haven't been thrown out of a job with little hope of finding another like so many people my age. And I'm grateful, too, that biting the hand that feeds me — mocking the system that keeps me in work — is somehow still possible. Luckily for me, "In the end everything is a gag," as Charlie Chaplin put it.

So, it's back to the drawing board while I still have a bone to pick.

Aislin

a.k.a. Terry Mosher

THE GODDAMN BOOK'S DONE! I'M HOME, CAROL... CAROL?